# Billy Goes to

## Harriet Cameron
## Illustrated by Karen Middleton

Hello! I'm Billy McNoo.
I'm going on an adventure, will you come too?

Billy, and his little dog Ben, waved goodbye to Haggis, the Highland cow, Iona, the Shetland pony and Skye the terrier who was Ben's best friend. They were going on an adventure to England. The two friends, Billy and Ben, wanted to watch the motorbike racing on the Isle of Man so they drove to Liverpool and caught the ferry across to the island.

The friends stood by the side of the road listening to the roar of the speeding motorbikes. Ben was a little bit frightened of the bikes whizzing past so close to him. But Billy held his little paw and Ben soon began to enjoy himself.

'Wow!' shouted Ben, 'those motorbikes are going as fast as rockets.'

Just then, one of the motorbikes pulled up next to them. The rider looked angry and upset. The strap holding the motorbike's battery had snapped. His battery was about to fall out. If he couldn't fix it quickly then he would not be able to win the race!

Billy looked at Ben and Ben looked at Billy. Ben quickly took off his smart, tartan collar and gave it to the rider. The rider used it to strap in the battery and then he raced off into the distance.

The next day Billy and Ben were out walking when they heard a shout. A man ran across the main road towards them. 'I won the race yesterday and it was all thanks to you!' he said, as he patted Ben gently on the head. 'Is there anything that I can do for you in return?' Billy looked at Ben, Ben looked at Billy. They both had the same idea!

The man fetched his powerful, red motorbike and the two
friends climbed on.  They had a great time zooming
around the Isle of Man.

Billy and Ben had really enjoyed their visit.  'I like
motorbikes now,' said Ben.

After taking the ferry back to Liverpool, Billy and Ben drove to Manchester. Billy bought two tickets, one for himself and one for Ben. They went to watch the Manchester United football team play at their home stadium, Old Trafford. Billy hadn't been to a football match before and he had been looking forward to seeing this match for a long time. Ben was excited too!

As they stood in the long queue to get into the stadium, Billy and Ben saw lots of interesting people. Some wore funny hats, some carried scarves and flags and some people even had their faces painted with red and black, the Manchester United colours. Billy decided to join in the excitement and bought himself a big hat.

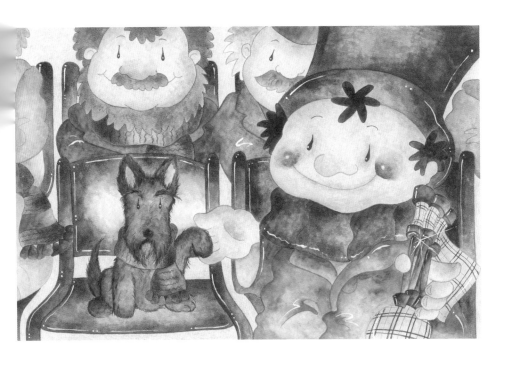

When Billy and Ben finally found their places Billy put his bagpipes under his seat and they sat waiting for the match to begin.

As the two teams came onto the pitch the crowds cheered and sang as loudly as they could. Little Ben started to bark and Billy picked him up so that he could see the match.

The whistle blew and the match began. The ball went this way and that way, but by half-time the teams hadn't scored a single goal. The crowds were disappointed but soon cheered up when they saw people selling hot dogs and drinks. Billy and Ben shared a big hotdog and the second half of the match began.

Manchester United were playing very well and were just about to score a goal, when the referee blew his whistle. Both teams stood around the football, with annoyed faces. Somebody in the crowd shouted that the football was going flat!

'Oh dear,' said Ben to Billy, 'what will they do now?' Then, Billy looked at Ben. 'I've got an idea,' he said. Billy bent down and pulled his bagpipes out from under his seat. 'Come with me Ben, we're going to help.' They went quickly down the steps and onto the pitch.

Billy gave his bagpipes to the referee who looked puzzled. But then Billy told him his idea. The referee joined the bagpipes to the football and started to pump it up. Before long the ball was as good as new.

Everyone was very grateful for Billy and Ben's help. The Manchester United Manager asked them to watch the rest of the match from his seat. They had the best seat in the stadium.

This was one of the greatest days out that Billy and Ben had ever had!

Billy and Ben jumped into their little, red car and drove further down into England, to Nottingham. They were going to visit Sherwood Forest, where the famous outlaw Robin Hood had once lived.

The two friends walked deep into the forest to see the Major Oak, a huge, hollow tree where Robin Hood used to hide from the Sheriff of Nottingham's soldiers. Ben had a look inside the tree. He jumped inside and hid from Billy. He was pretending to be Robin Hood. Suddenly an owl, sitting in the top of the tree, hooted. Poor little Ben nearly jumped out of his skin and he quickly ran back to Billy.

Just then a lady in a blue coat ran up to Billy and Ben.
She was crying. 'Have you seen a little boy?  My little boy
has got lost in the forest.'
'No we haven't,' said Billy, 'I'm very sorry.'  Billy thought
for a minute and then he looked at Ben. 'I've got an idea,'
he said, 'have you got anything that belongs to your little
boy?'
'Yes,' said the lady, 'I've got my little boy's gloves in my
pocket.'

Billy gave the gloves to Ben who sniffed them with his little, black nose. Ben knew what to do. He ran back along the footpath where the lady had been, until he could smell the little boy's scent. Ben followed the little boy's scent into the forest. The lady and Billy ran after him. Soon they heard the sound of crying in the distance. Sitting at the bottom of a tree was the little boy. The lady rushed to the little boy and picked him up.

'How can I ever thank you enough?' asked the lady. Billy looked at Ben and Ben looked at Billy. They were both very hungry. The lady smiled. Soon the friends were sitting in the café, eating a big plate of bangers and mash. 'Having a good sense of smell can be very useful,' said Ben as he tucked into his meal.

Billy and Ben got back into their little car. Their next adventure was going to be in the capital of England, London.

When the friends arrived in London, they went straight to the Houses of Parliament to see where all the Members of Parliament meet to make England's laws.

'What a huge building,' said Billy to Ben. 'Did you know that there's a Ben here that's much bigger than you and it makes a much louder noise!'

Ben looked puzzled until Billy told him that Big Ben was the name of the bell in the clock tower.

Next, they went to 10 Downing Street to see where the Prime Minister lives.

After that they caught a big, red, London bus which took them to Buckingham Palace, the home of the Queen.

They stood at the tall, black railings and watched the Changing of the Guard.

Billy and Ben noticed a guardsman throwing a ball for some corgis to fetch. He threw the ball too hard and it bounced through the railings. Ben caught the ball in his mouth and he passed it back through the railings to one of the corgi dogs.

'Thank you very much,' said the corgi, 'who are you?'
'I'm Ben and I'm from Scotland.'
'It's the Scots Guards who are on duty here at the
moment,' said the corgi, 'I'm sure they would love to meet
a dog from Scotland.' Ben climbed through the Palace
railings and the corgi took him to meet the Scots Guards
who made a big fuss of him and gave him some sweets.

Next the corgi took Ben on a tour of the Palace. He saw
lots of different rooms and the maids and the footmen
were all very kind to him. 'You mustn't go in that room,'
warned the corgi, 'the Queen is in there having her tea.'
But Ben couldn't resist having a little peep around the
door. The Queen was eating roast beef and Yorkshire
pudding.

When Ben had finished looking around, the corgi took him
back outside to where Billy was still waiting. 'Where have
you been?' asked Billy.
'I've been on a tour of the Palace,' said Ben. Billy wanted
to hear all about it.

Their next journey was a long one. Very long. Too long for little Ben. 'Are we nearly there yet?' he asked. 'Yes,' said Billy, 'here we are now at Lands End.' Billy and Ben climbed out of their little car and walked to the edge of the cliffs. The cliffs were very steep and so Billy carried Ben whilst they looked out over the sea.

Billy saw a small crowd of people. They were having their photographs taken next to a signpost. The man taking the photographs asked Billy where he lived. He quickly changed the name on the signpost so that it showed Billy's hometown and the distance to it from Lands End. Billy and Ben smiled for the camera. 'What a lovely way to remind us of our visit,' said Billy to Ben. Ben wagged his tail happily.

As the two friends were walking to get a nice cup of tea, they saw a man bending down near some rocks. He looked upset. 'Can you help?' he asked, 'I'm a coach driver and when I was taking my hanky out of my pocket the coach keys came out too. They have fallen down between these two rocks and my hand is too big to fit down the gap.' Billy tried to help, but his hand was also too big.

Ben tried to reach the keys with his paw, but he couldn't reach the shiny, silver coloured keys either. They all stood, thinking. Billy looked at Ben and Ben looked at Billy. 'I've got an idea,' said Billy. He took his bagpipes off his back. He put one of the pipes down between the rocks. Then, instead of blowing like he normally did, he began to suck. The keys stuck to the end of the pipe, Billy lifted the pipe out from between the rocks and gave the coach keys back to the driver.

'Thank you,' said the driver, 'I am taking some American tourists around England in that coach and without you they wouldn't have been going any further!'

The coach driver bought Billy and Ben a lovely Cornish cream tea, as a way of saying thank you. While they were having their tea, the American tourists from the coach came into the café.

Billy and Ben chatted to the American tourists. They liked Billy's tartan kilt. They told Billy and Ben how much they were enjoying touring England. 'Have you ever been abroad?' one American asked Billy.

'No, never,' said Billy. Billy looked at Ben and Ben looked at Billy. 'Perhaps our next adventure could be to visit a country abroad.' Ben wagged his tail and barked! It sounded a good idea to him too.

We've had an adventure and learnt lots of things new.
Have you?

# LISTENING TO READERS

Billy and Ben saw lots of animals on their adventures around England.

Can you find them?

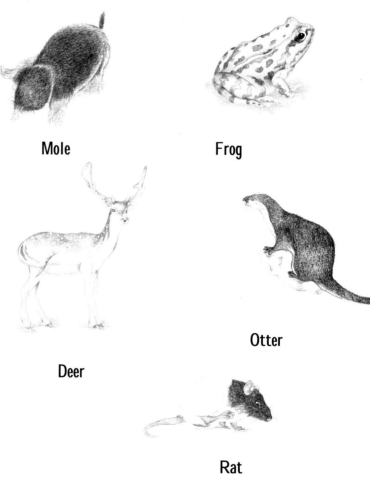

Mole

Frog

Deer

Otter

Rat

# Listening to Readers

- **Reading should be a pleasure.** It should be fun! Children who are enjoying their reading will learn far more. Your child should not be made to feel that they have failed to read something. Emphasise the positive. Remember your child has read 90 out of 100 words correctly and not failed to read 10 words!

- **Take opportunities to praise.** Do not correct every word that your child misreads. Wait until the end of the page. Praise them for reading the whole page and longer words that they have correctly read. Then go back to one or two words that you feel that they should have read correctly but didn't. Point to the word and say, 'Have another try at this word.'

While reading with your child you may wish to point out some of the following:

- **Simile:** A simile compares one thing to another. For example: As cold as ice. Can your child find an example of a simile on page 3?

- **Vowels and consonants:** Choose a word and ask your child to identify these. Vowels are A, E, I, O, U (Y can be either a vowel or consonant). All the other letters are consonants. All words have a vowel in them.

- **Punctuation:** Remember that full stops indicate a pause and commas indicate a shorter pause.

- **Onomatopoeia:** Words that sound like the things that they are describing. For example: bang, cluck, quack and moo. Can your child find three onomatopoeic words on page 3?

- **Homonym:** Words that sound the same but have a different meaning. For example: roar and raw, way and weigh, their and there. Can your child find an example on page 7?

- **Meanings beyond the literal:** For example: It's raining cats and dogs, or pull your socks up. Can your child find an example on page 16?

- **Alliteration:** When words next to each other begin with the same sound. For example: the deep, dark ocean or the scaly, scary dragon. Can your child find examples on pages 16 and 29?

During and after reading this book with your child you may wish to discuss some of the following:

- **Making predictions:** Stop your child reading at certain places throughout the book. Ask them what they think is about to happen. Some good places to stop are at the bottom of pages 4, 11 and 17.

- **Sequencing:** Ask your child to put the places that Billy and Ben visited into the correct order.

- **Summarising:** At the end of each adventure you could ask your child to tell you, in their own words, what had happened in the adventure.

- **Describing a character:** Ask your child to describe a character from the story.

- **Feelings of characters:** Ask your child how they think that the coach driver felt when he lost his keys or how the little boy felt when he had lost his mother.

- **Asking questions:** When asking a child questions about the book avoid asking questions which can result in a yes or no answer. Some good questions would be, 'How did the motorcycle racer, on the Isle or Man, repay Billy and Ben for their help?' or, 'Where else could Billy and Ben visit?' 'Why do you think that they would enjoy going there?'

Billy and Ben saw lots of animals on their adventures around England.

Can you find them?

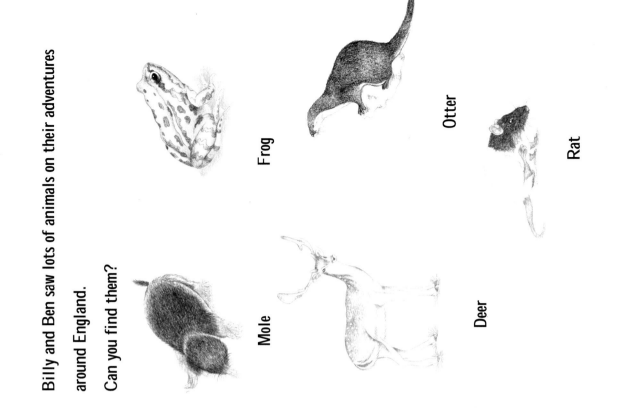

Frog

Otter

Rat

Mole

Deer

34